HYMNS TO PHENOMENA

HYMNS TO PHENOMENA

S. D. JOHNSON

THISTLEDOWN PRESS

© S.D. Johnson, 2000
All rights reserved

No part of this publication may be reproduced or transmitted in any form or by any means, graphic, electronic or mechanical, including photocopying, recording, or any information storage and retrieval system, without permission in writing from the publisher. Requests for photocopying of any part of this book shall be directed in writing to CanCopy, 6 Adelaide Street East, Suite 900, Toronto, Ontario, M5C 1H6.

Canadian Cataloguing in Publication Data

Johnson, Sherry, 1972 –
Hymns to phenomena
Poems.
ISBN 1-894345-15-0
PS8569.O36927 H9 2000   C811'.54   C00-920173-4
PR9199.3.J596 H9 2000

Cover graphic, *A Game of Chess* by S. D. Johnson
Cover and book design by Jackie Forrie
Typeset by Thistledown Press Ltd.
Printed and bound in Canada

Thistledown Press Ltd.
633 Main Street
Saskatoon, Saskatchewan
S7H 0J8

Canadian Heritage   Patrimoine canadien

Thistledown Press gratefully acknowledges the financial assistance of the Canada Council for the Arts, the Saskatchewan Arts Board, and the Government of Canada through the Book Publishing Industry Development Program for its publishing program.

*— for you —*

TABLE OF CONTENTS

LESSONS FOR THE BODY

    I. *Colour*      10
    II. *Beauty*      12
    III. *Geometry*      13
    IV. *Space*      14
    V. *Metaphor*      15
    VI. *Sound*      17
    VII. *Gravity*      18
    VIII. *The Soul*      20

IN THE RIND

    *fovea centralis*      24
    But Quietly      25
    *Fabula Cygnorum*      27
    I Shall Never Describe      29
    Goosefoot and Plantain      31
    In the Rind      33
    Through Light      35

MOSTLY NOUGHT

    Stones      38
    Two Magpies      41
    Virus      42
    A Short Gothic Tale      45
    Mr. Cogito Investigates
        the Edge of Everything      48
    Instructions for October      49

*Liber Ecstatis*                           52

THE WAY METAL IS BORN

Outdoor Chess                              62
Private History of the Drone               64
Coelacanth                                 68
Soliloquy of the Housefly                  72
In Praise of Metal                         74


AN OMNIGRAVIS

*Omnigravis*                          80
The Fulcrum of Flight                 83
Half Unfolded                         85
Rodin's *Eve*                         87
*The Nativity*                        89
The Hermit                            91
*Rosa Animae*                         93

NOTES AND ACKNOWLEDGEMENTS        95

*Nor was I hungry — so I found
That Hunger — was a way
Of Persons outside Windows —
The Entering — takes away —*

— Emily Dickinson




*in dead earnest
offer to the betrayed world
a rose*
— Zbigniew Herbert

LESSONS FOR THE BODY

I. *Colour*

        All events in the history of matter are known
to the angel of black —
        Savant, with a mind
        of pure memory, he lives
in chambers beneath the earth, — his body
so burdened with jewels, and possessed
of such massive girth

his wings flex uselessly: —

                His burrow a torrent
of bright objects, procured by admirers —
All gifts are accepted by him, —
he collects everything.


The eye, — always hopelessly in love
with an absence. Everything not held —

        (The angel of yellow
wears robes of blue —
the angel of cyan
is swathed in red . . . )


This is not glamour though, as it appears
but a form of compassion — what is needed
                is taken, the eye
devouring what remains —
with its cormorant appetite.


        The angel of white
needs nothing at all,
is naked. One of the cosmos' last ascetics.

I once conversed
with the angel of white, —
                         his gaunt body
    pendulous, feet
pointed skyward, — like the roots
of the tree of life.

He had beauteous goat eyes.
And after a time, he descended into speech
so abstract
it was entirely lacking in objects: —


I was very moved by him, — but left with a feeling
of intercostal loneliness —


I couldn't embrace him when we parted,
    for the wind tossed
his body askance

*Ah but I am so very thin,* he said
*my isn't*
*bruises your what*

*No mattering: —*
*I unfold and unfold*

*I flower,*
        *I rose*
*the endless expansing*

*be wary*
*of my isn't*

*the not*
*of my dancing . . .*

II. *Beauty*

Machine of perpetual desire
What leads you to walk far away from everything

        To find a quiet almost-empty room
Where you sit with sorrow turning on its lathe

To find the heart's fontanel still tender,
*Who walked between the violet and the violet*

Tender the prayer spoken for another, and moments of silence
Why do bees live in a world where red is an absence

        What makes you fall on your knees weeping with ecstasy
When you have abandoned ten thousand masters

Master, you beg of it, regard me in a moment of silence
*Who walked between the violet and the violet*

III. *Geometry*

The first lesson is the point.

        But what is drawn on the page,
a lie, — you can't
build it,
        or tear it apart

You can't go to battle against it —
or court it donning feathers,
or with a song.

        Because like anything existing
            entirely in the mind,
it moves beyond you —
            like the meaning of a speech uttered
by a spider in the grass,
        through her funnel of vertigoes

like breath on a swing

In the end all form is incomprehensible, —
            to fathom its hypostasis
is to descend deeply
into the hero's eye, —

to pull
and tauten yourself
along eternity

        to throw yourself headlong
into time

to be heroic like time: — dying
as you are born.

IV. *Space*

In speculations of the beginning
it prevails, an endless loge

                where God sits waiting
for the phenomenal opera to begin unfolding

But maybe matter was the first event, its infinitely dense weight
surrounding God in his infancy —
a *blankie Dei*.

                And then God
opening phenomena's curtains, —

*Fiat spatium!*

Because space is as much a miracle
as matter or light,
or anything —

It isn't
a mere backdrop — a badly-painted,
expendable landscape
or a stock character

                Without it
there is no backdrop —

nor play nor actors

                Everything becoming
the stage's horizon, where the players
and the audience converge,
in pursuit of one another —

but all of them are missing.

V. *Metaphor*

You want to write a poem underwater,
                                  for the metaphor to take
a long time to reach you

to see beyond the spiny skeletons of glass,
beyond their fans and intricate
baskets,
        or hydras

their heads thrown back
in saintly postures

You want to believe
in solitudes of nuclei,
                    what simple intent

you want to behold the heart
deserving such fantastic homage

a cross-sectional view, —
        with the surface never lost — you would have
                                        its ascent slowed
this being
swimming towards you

which is this,
which is also that

      This and that
clasped together
not like lovers

but like a cell
   on the brink

releasing a permutation to the world

And what binds
each piece together yet

is the sound of praise

for that which cleaves them

That which cleaves them is known in the body
in its billion privacies, asunder
from the mind's logic

Metaphor is understood and born
as naturally
as a bed of oysters chanting the time

      They measure the time
honestly

  — by the breadth of their pearls.

VI. *Sound*

It is the threshold of touch,
                bridging an expanse
yet remaining bound, — then what is almost grasped
recasts the gesture

a living mirror: —

or, the port de bras of the beloved
and the beloved.

Hysteric, — somewhat
tangible,
        but like a factory
where what is in the world is taken apart

                and then reassembled
into that which is absolute form, — like bees

propelling themselves into the sun,
                returning to flowers not of the earth
but ones that exist
within the walls of poetry
alone.

        Like words immolated
into sheer meaning,
                what is sound
but the air
adoring itself —

        its love of the hallucination
of whatever it believes
itself to be.

VII. *Gravity*

Inventor of the interval, —
                       the hands
that hold the epoch,
               spinning
in its exhausted confusion
of space

               What is fathomed most
in the sculptor's heart

that lithic anvil, —
               which bares itself
to inherit a fantasie of hammers, —
a queue of hammers

veiled in medieval lace

               He has seen the imperishable light
cast from the manifold, unsheltered bodies

               and knows its deliverance
will fashion
such grief-stricken crags along the flesh

flesh that falls
continually as a ransom, — to a space
conceived for its presence —

               until what is left
falls after pitch and hew of stone,
                         flesh
realized into stone

      until camber of foot and breast
are levelled on some axis of the mind

and he can only look
at statue,
        at naked flesh

        and only wonder what as yet
unborn star
they live on

VIII. *The Soul*

> *Before the full*
> *it sought itself and afterwards the world.*
> — Owen Aherne (via W.B. Yeats)

      White wingless bird, on a branch which juts
outside the bourne of time —

Around it, a landscape scored with improbabilities —
                              its satellites
chiseled from salt,
and ice and metals

                              — a sun
dispelling numbers: — which settle gently
their radiance upon its world.


The bird is so beautiful, to cast one's eyes upon it
is sure annihilation —

                      like the ophanim, the angels
who wheel momentarily around God — but then, because
of their intense admiration, are obliterated
by the time they mouth the third *sanctus*: —

The bird dreams of Eden, —
of the invention of flesh, —

           To pass the time
it sings hymns to phenomena.

Praying for wings, — desiring to be
    among the roots, which seem
an impossible distance below

>         But just as the bird
is everywhere, in all bodies, phenomena buries
its roots deeply within it —
and there is no end to it.

Just look around you and you will know.

Phenomena is everywhere.

IN THE RIND

FOVEA CENTRALIS

I place you in the company of owls,
with their meta-human faces —

      the kingdom of dead suns behind
every immovable eye

          I veil my body
            with the broken flesh
of pine and juniper, to be
the forest to which you must return

      But O, to go with you
on that other flight,
                as you plummet towards
the thing you most need

hunter with one thought,
                repeating itself
endlessly in the gullet

          Even in the dark
I would be in your eye's centre, —
as it pulls around the light.

BUT QUIETLY

      The rain has many quiet chambers
in which I contemplate you —
                          because it's a body
which makes one intimate with distance

Enclosed in what goes on for miles
I find such silence
thinking of your voice,
                hooded in blue
and white-hearted rain

        Among these hearts my own
is whelmed in many voices

but it beats quietly,

   like a piano hammer
falling into empty space

                — air where the string is long broken —

It has moved against your absence for years.
It finds nothing,
but keeps falling there anyway

I feel nearer to you now than I ever have
in the shelter of the weeping osier

                                        In my arms
how private her mind is — her mind
        is like that of a woman
searching a crowd for her lover

This waiting is everything to her,
as she stands unnoticed in the throng
thinking only of his voice,
of her grey skirt

and beneath its dark folds
her gift

her garters of bees

FABULA CYGNORUM

Gibbous moon, *luna saltatoris*
humming Chopin,
                      hetero-poise with the stars
like the breast of a killdeer, — on the verge
of falling over

I walk through trees obscuring the city —
spring trees in their elementary shapes,
                      but everything with a handprint
                      of green paint
in the apex of its mind.

As I walk I say a prayer to your face —
        because it allows time
to lie broken beneath my feet

                through its pieces
the roses of absence spring forth: —
                      shedding footsteps and lost keys
as they arrive
— footsteps and lost keys — as they spin
their thin bodies
out of the earth, —

I am in love with your absence.  It allows desire
                      to twist itself
into every possible shape.

Because it makes me believe each star
is the light of a swan

adrift in a coracle

Nestled tightly into its afterlife
on a brood of eggs,
     all of them white
     as an imago's mind

Eggs which can be opened
and closed
like lockets

    In each one the rising
and falling of an earthly desire, —

If one is opened and observed
for only a moment,
     it is enough
to ponder for a century.

Stars are swans
which have drifted into the afterworld

     sitting quietly at their oars
pondering earthly love, listening for the far-off
murmuring of desire —
     the faint light
drifting in from another story

over the wall of its boat,
     and the deeper wall of dark.

I SHALL NEVER DESCRIBE

      Of course I used to implicate your mouth
in some of the grandest events of history, —
when I would imagine
the first maker of wine,
                      it was your lips
to which the cup was raised

upon all anonymous figures, those
      who somehow carried
brightness into the world

the inventor of fire: — that first
glassblower in Sidonia: —

Upon them all love, I imposed your mouth —
and behind it always was the wraith of your absent
and terribly beautiful face.

It is only for you I have had enduring love.
      After the many pretenders,
I have had enough folly, — I have forsaken
my paint, all postures —

— my scarves and jewellry.

                    My love for you has become
almost nothing — though I still dream of giving you
many impossible things, — I want to crown you
with a garland of metamorphoses

or gather roses the colour of blood
flowing over a swan: —

I shall never describe the way you touched me.

Not because I am incapable,
but because it would be wrong.

I can't say very much about it, only
that I believe that wherever you are
................from the beginning of time
my heart has moved with yours,
like one millstone
with another

................and when I think of your touch
I feel like a mirror leaning against a wall
in the dark of an empty closet —

Because after many years it is only the belief
in itself that remains.
And how empty it is of anything else.

O, it is the only pure thing!
It has no more meaning than a stone.

It is utterly immaculate.

## GOOSEFOOT AND PLANTAIN

For days I dig the weed plat
        sowing flowers and vegetables
where only weeds have grown

most of the weeds are thrown away,
                                  but some are fashioned
into a wild salad —
goosefoot and plantain

small piles of weeds
to deepen my poverty,
                a poverty
I fall on my knees to

because sometimes it holds me in its arms
and burnishes me clean —
                because only when I am happy with almost nothing
will I be ready for the beloved, and only then
will there be room for his arrival.

For days I have been digging,
        uncovering the transparent
incandescence of worms

like small trains pushing through the soil,
                                  each with a furnace
churning earth into light,
earth into light

From the trees I'm watched
by those seasonless, nipple-coloured birds
                each with a hallux piercing
my heart with their slight quietude

How small and modest they are,
how devoted —
                they are like slaves
                who stay with you
though the cupboard might be bare,
though all winter
it was bare


                Their patience is the patience
I am gathering for the beloved,
as I sow the earth
        with what might fail

I wait for the beloved to come to me,
                        as I eat
what would have rotted in the ground
or been thrown away

        I fill my mouth with his poverty. I am astounded
beyond speech at his beauty, and would wait
years to have him,
                for him to come to me
with nothing

— which is perfection —
                what is only
essential, — after years of not having anything,
it is that one thing offered to me
that I can't refuse.

IN THE RIND


I cradle my face in the tree's roots, —
        to hear your heart fluttering
deep within the bole

       I am learning to find you
in the smallest things —
hidden in things,
               because it's where your presence gathers

       what remains of you
around the spaces where you walk,
         in chambers
you enter
and pass through


            I have no choice
but to live in the smallest things, —
because when I think of your mouth
and look at a lemon polished in light

each of its pores
seems as wide as a country

In your mouth
and your mouth's memory,
               I am ensconced in attentions: —

I find myself in a doorway —
the threshold of a descending stair —

Your mouth precedes me, drawing me
down through the intraphysicum.

Here where at the end of everything
         is your tongue
folding me in rind.

Here where everywhere is the rind.

## THROUGH LIGHT

In autumn the last imagos, in their singular monomania for romance, essay to mate with falling, dying leaves. Apparently in lab experiments, if a stroboscope oscillates at an appropriate rhythm, the male throws itself into the pulse — striving to do nothing less than to mate with light.

I think maybe this is how I would describe my movement towards the beloved — whose body to me is more impetus than form.

I have been mistaken thinking love can exist because of someone's hands, or the sound of a voice alone.

It is not only the sound of your voice, but its rhythm, and the way your mouth arranges vowels so they wax and wane in a manner I understand—in the sense that it somehow is aligned with the cadence of my own language.

And though your hands are lovely, possessing so many bones, it is not the hands I love, but their motions — this is their radiance, their measure in time.

When I look at your hands they make light astonishing. I don't know what else I can say, because anything else would be music, or maybe a language I'd like to invent with you consisting entirely of vowels: —

*Tibi inter tempum cantavi. Per lucem.*
    *In orem meum nominem tuum*
*aveo ponere.*

*— Sed ubivis est.*

*O claritas absentiae:*
*lucem tuum intravi —*

I shall mate with your light.

MOSTLY NOUGHT

STONES

Scholars of silence, of cosmography
and eschatology

       All stones labour quietly to re-establish themselves
as citizens of pure phenemona —

To be phenemona of a perdurable rind.
Barely discernable from without, but from within

       mirror upon mirror: — an architectonic
of ever involutions.

Needless to say, it is difficult
to understand their conversations . . .

———•———

Early in their histories, stones
free-fell through myriad cultures, —

       But alas, stones
       move through a culture

as if it were gossamer, and have
utter contempt for it

for all politics, —
religions and institutions.

       Never interrogate
a stone for a solution.

Their language, wholly consonants, disassembled
       and then regathered into speech

of inconceivable density, has almost
never been heard, —

      When you pick one up and query it
its utterances fall away into the grass, — the soil —

into the lines of the palm.
      Where an inevitable part of your destiny

              is to never on earth
have access to the speech of stones.

———•—•———

Stones, — most immaculate vehicles
of pure thought.

Their lives are devoted to the construction
of one syllogism

              (the sole thing
in which stones have solidarity)

              composed
of an infinite number of parts: —

Its conclusion?
To not have one.

This is what stones finally
propose a toast to —

              at banquets
in their own particular paradise.

                   Their glasses
overflowing with gravity, — which they imbibe

until it pulls them back to the world again.
They go along, letting it take them

where it will — where
they are born among other stones

              with a pain
something like a hangover.

And they resume their labours again,
              moiling upon their one syllogism

midnight and dawn, but with
eternity slightly altered: —

Their ecstasy is sustained by the occult essence
they perceive at the heart of phenemona.

They have never seen it, or spoken to it
in myriad infinities —

But not once have they faltered
in their belief in its existence

so they can sit thinking perpetually, — with their minds never once straying far from the arms of song.

TWO MAGPIES

Two magpies
on the river's edge, —
                    one carcass of seagull.

            They're like nuns
thrown out of the convent, —
heartling chortily.

The river drags its memory over stones,
                            haling away from them
something of their time: —

        I want to lie here like this forever, or at least
until a quiet overtakes me, — and grass
grows up through my mind.

The gull is meat, — its mother
is oblivion.

The sisters nod and nod, the gull
is good food.

They're tearing it
into pieces of heaven.

VIRUS

I.

You might consider me the netherside of Byzantium
with my spiny dome, and my heart
                          a helical staircase

          Know my brides
are waiting in your cells, —

your clear-eyed cells

You want to know
if I have a mind, or what my mind is —

             My mind is like a chess game
on the periodic table — that last row
with the ones beyond it,
                      on the page's white

The untold elements
you could never understand,
with those tiles polished
                    so brightly

their explosions

burnished beyond sight

II.

But I'm simple too,
               just a maw
spinning in an empty locule,
     an appetite searching
for a tenement among nerves

           the blue palace in your blood

I was your fear of the gypsy camp,
     impelling your hand to whip your horse
     so your carriage could hasten through

Like them, I find contentment in the journey —
happy in a vat of swine's tears, or a vaulting flea

     I carry a bag
of finery and appellations,
               delighted in a Tartar

               travelling from continent to continent

Though I'm vagrant I am a tendency
     towards repose, — the still point
at the centre of the fulcrum,
               and the desire
in its arms for stillness

My harem is waiting in your cells — I'll build it
mating with myself, breeding over and over
with myself

This because a weight needs to be carried away
and I will carry you away

I am only you: —
so be still in my arms, beloved

Throw your head back
and I will whisper to you
all of my secrets

*The dead are motionless
and yet turning below the earth —
you, who are bride and cathedral
seed and flower*

*Like a stone
you are the darling of gravity*

— *Both orbit and star* —

A SHORT GOTHIC TALE

The night without periphery,
        like an endless descent
into a border of mourning paper

the dark is musk-dispelling and mysterious, —
it goes on and on,
twisted and many-cambered, like the hair
of a governess, —

You want to possess the pins which fasten it, pins
you might bury beneath the forest floor,
        and dig up again

to mount a collection of rare bees, perhaps

or to prick your flesh letting blood for a signature, —
entering a contract declaring loyalty
to a society of owls, —

        The moon is like her waning face
bent over a candle

        a flexion of bone
cutting shadow from light —

(she spends her evenings now
sipping laudanum)

        She is becoming very tired
of being intact amidst all the ruin —

because things are so bizarre in the castle
she wants desperately to keep hold of her sanity, —

(and maybe the only way
sanity can be preserved
is to learn to imagine
anything, — )

Ghosts wander her room and the edge of sleep
attired in fashions of a previous century

she thinks of them merely as lost, —
with their mouths composed
of dropped stitches

they are bits of misplaced time

To her the children are what is *really* frightening,
they way they all have the same wooden face
but each a different height

as if all together they composed
a set of *matreshka*

She met them this morning on the staircase,
each in an identical white nightgown
one by one floating over the bannister

      and she brushed them away
like strands of untidy hair

five girls drifting back over the rail,
each grabbing a tear-shaped crystal
                on the chandelier

except the toddler who laughed
and swung from toe to toe

   twenty feet in the air —

The governess laughs too,
a genius at fear

ready to believe
the everything
and all

     she walks to breakfast
with her shoes laced with half-crossed thresholds,
no longer distinguishing
between the real,
         the imagined treacheries

she laughs and descends the long staircase —
wrapping herself tightly
    in a hypnagogic shawl

## MR. COGITO INVESTIGATES THE EDGE OF EVERYTHING

First he sends the raven out
to the edge of infinity
the raven gets lost     vanishes
against the black endless fabric

the silk of the void believing
it is part of its mind

He sends columba next
pale    like a shadow's shadow
columba returns

with death in her mouth

*It's not what I'm looking for*
he tells columba
angrily he shakes her
small body like a bottle of champagne

*Go back*
*to the edge of things*
*bring me a branch or a drop of blood*
*gather a stone     a dead flower*

*fly around the edge*
*until you can bring me something other than this*

*or until you die columba*

INSTRUCTIONS FOR OCTOBER

Admire the trees, because they divulge the same mood as an exhibit
of Magdelanian paintings, —
and the late asters — the only thing with petals remaining
in the doe-coloured grasses, — Bend your ear
to their compassionate songs.
Their sermon to the field about poverty.

      The only thing to do now in the afternoons
is to walk far away from the city —
Wear a torn dress. And wander until you find
an abandoned building.

Bring a delicate china cup, beige with orange flowers
and crack it against the wall, —
and then sit for hours, among fragments of glass, porcelain doll parts,
scraps of mouldy cloth, — a worn bridle for a horse
      sunk long ago into the pasture — and be in awe

        of the silence which can only unfold
among things that are broken.

Expect the dead to come, — near dark
when mist overtakes the fields —
Laden with sorrow, they are afraid the angel of life
      will forget them, not assemble for them
new pairs of hands to rearrange their phenomena —

Praise the wind of bodiless wings.
Hold the dead in your arms, and assure them that what is
is mostly nought, — mostly poverty.

Let the hour rest for once,
and wear its own apparel.

Let the word be what is passing.

*LIBER ECSTATIS*

LIBER ECSTATIS
(for Cory)

> So the ruby has nothing engraved on it!
> It doesn't need markings.
>
> — Rumi

I.

The spider detests this house,
                        its customary rooms

She is bored with a simple geometry —
and practising her handwriting,
                        that script
which by now is immaculate

with all eight limbs

She contemplates a room she has never beheld,
its walls a multitude of angles —
                        white
multiplying itself on white

a perspective

wide as a supplication

This to furnish a space between flies,
                        imagining a room
which moves infinitely, like a blind dancer

She waits for the moon to rise into the window, —
                              with its cinematography
                              of curves and tea

It is the only change she tolerates
                far removed through the gridiron

its pattern predictable — all of its shapes
are known.

II.

Each fly's death is a luxury —
envy a silk death-cradle

Her lullaby,
        with its octave of reds

        its attending hallucinations

            They have no fear
of being inhaled into her face

to plunge into a countenance
of well-oiled hinges,
        manifold eyes

        because it's the way a face might be
        if one were orchestrated
from moieties of an angel's wings

Her voice is a boat,
        taking them
to that place they have always longed for

a boat filled with opium and orange rinds,
                bearing them home
to their name swaddled in indigo

wearied of a shifting world,
        a life

vistas entirely of fragments

They row themselves slowly into her mouth,
                                            they say goodnight
happy
to finally be going somewhere

                They wave farewell to what they leave on land
a smudge of glue and some gauzy husks —
                                    a final bonfire
of costumes

                *sleep*

                *sleep*

sings the spider, — *I will*
*carry you through beauty*

III.

She never strays far
              from a cornice above the stairs

people ascending and descending,
                            their faces
like tides forgetting
where the moon is

Of their waste she makes a vocation —
its enticement for flies

It's not that she is indolent, —
                            she just can't stray far
with each lung a tattered parchment,
                                she sits waiting
                                    like an invalid
with a bottle of poison

Bit of conversation
drifting
    along a beam of light and dust

                They speak of chaos at the dinner table

They live in a jail of rhetoric, —
                            it filigrees
a large space between them,
                        an invented disorder

                    Their wafts of vowels  
surge constantly into her air,  
          which she traverses on an invisible portico

She sorts them into those that are meaningless  
and the other occasional vowels

These she writes into a book of ecstasy,  
                              with a stylus of breath

the pages of words uttered  
by those who forget they are speaking

IV.

*This room is my death*, she thinks,
                              *this room*
                          *where the form of the walls*
*are so perfect, they would be spoiled by any painting*

*where solitude empties its arms*
*and clasps its own two hands together, wound firmly*
           *around a conclusion*, —

*Death polishes loneliness.*
*It carves a form for it* —
                    *graceful and still*
                    *as Cassiopeiae, death*
*gives patience a throne* —

*I will sit in this chamber,*
            *around the edge of time and space*

*infinite in its white motion,*
*the infinite which is without*
*statement* —
*or judgement* —

*My death is not grace then:* —
                  *it will be to open*
*one of many shutters, and in that frame*

                  *a revenant of grace*

*Grace falling towards me*
*through eternity: —*

    *through the cores of planets*
*crying from joy*
*in the preternatural darkness*

*in the nurseries of stars*

*My death is paradise, —*
                            *it is simply a mind forever*

*on the verge of its event*

# THE WAY METAL IS BORN

OUTDOOR CHESS

The days cubing themselves on green,
                                        begonias spreading
their glamourous fans

        their one heart
a slow cadence,
                pumping inside a stone.

Dragonflies, two and two, —
        their thin bodies
like mullions, bracing windows
                      into every other world

You would to drown an air of fragments: —
Playing chess in the garden,
                where the fence arranges
and rearranges its umbrage
all day

The dragonflies are Templars
                — ghosts in blue armour

        the trees heavy with ripe apples
but also sere remains of another season, — dead fruit
                      like refugees admiring
the last object of value they possess, a silver cup
or scrap of handmade lace

          Light falling sideways
among tangled vines and runners,
                 you are a transmyriad
of the flesh of the garden, — you believe
you could move through anything,
                         in the middle
                         of the L-shaped afternoon.

PRIVATE HISTORY OF THE DRONE

I.

I was born in the immaculate hexagon,
                              in a queue of white stars
rooms fashioned by my sisters

their slender, barren waists

They drew wax from the secret furnaces,
                                    expanding the hive
because this was their singular legacy

        and I watched in awe of them, these prodigies of design
I, who was born so helpless

I was born without legs or wings

still they fed me bread and honey —
they were so beautiful, combing pollen from their hair


II.

I never questioned the darkness, or their absence
                                    my chamber sealed
with what they pulled from their bodies

and so I could smell their sweet smell
in my loneliness, as I found my own fire

as I became what I would become

Pupa, profound will in the fire

forge in the Permian heart

fire hammering skeleton and wings, will
imploding into the loins


III.

My mind was almost nothing,
— a meagre space between locked wings —
and so I wandered the hive like a ghost,
                              with little to occupy me
waiting for my beautiful sisters, the honey in their mouths

young queen and old queen playing chess


Young queen with the ultraviolet mind,
              old queen with torn wings, reverent lace
incapable of flight

conductors of the measure, architects of the unlimited equation —
                    single drone in the hive
understanding little, waiting for destiny
to submit among the combs
              or a teacher within the pride

              a brief unlocking of my wings

to have assemblies of pure potential —
                    engraving inexhaustible
avenues along my eyes.

IV.

My sisters made a circle around young queen
murder in her hair, bloodpools along her baskets

the hive gathered silent around her

She lectured on love and necessity, how
they were the same thing

and I finally understood my destiny
what it was I would become,
                    as she gyrated her abdomen in the air

I followed her on her flight, in that season
of dying flowers

my magnum opus

        placing a million daughters
on the forge

and sunlight on our bodies

        the breath of that many wings
opening and closing


V.

I never questioned my sisters,
tearing me to pieces with their barbs
              living as I did
beyond my purpose

my maw a slag in the white order

Surely I was dying a god, with the legion
     of kingdoms I would inherit, the million empty stars
waiting to be filled

how many legacies, ripping my body to pieces
                        their own bodies falling
all around me

How I loved them, even then, —

     how could I not grieve
for the very stars,
             O my genius sisters

for the snow inside your mouths.

COELACANTH

I.

Blue-green and violet nailed with silver,
white Devonian caul over my eyes

      I breathe an inscrutable prayer shawl
over the reef

To unassembled questions, —
                        the god
of half-formed things,
deep in my chrysalis heart

meso-being: —
in the hot mouth of the athanor


district of the hysteric moon

Waltz with me then,
                in the unassembled question, —
between firmly-rooted locations,
in the midst of chaos

their lodgings fast
on the threshold of infinity


for four hundred million years, I have danced here.

II.

I never wanted transformation,
blind execution of my will

       but sought simply
to observe, —

              refracted as I was
              in the mouths of everything

I never wanted the sun falling directly into my body, —

       I wanted it perfumed
with air and water

       — because in the sky
I could never swim
through such looms of emptiness

wefting
and unwefting

             O to move
through such widespread

— panicles of light —

III.

No lapidary on the moon,
                        nor passage through the fabric

I am simply a hammer, —

— half-way fallen through the air —

lifted carefully before it strikes

Listen then,
because I have known such visions here

of those who crawled ashore,
                        pied
in bright, dangerous colours

— and I know of that other fire,
       the fire
which would simply burn me —

So waltz with me,
in the unassembled question, — you
whose hands I have seen

                    in that light
at the end of the world

That sorrow of light I have spoken to,
                              and comforted

as it fell into darkness

tired pinpoints of light,
exhausted
in so little time

having mined so hard for love, —
                              the terrible journeys they made

into darkness

into every human eye

SOLILOQUY OF THE HOUSEFLY

So they caught me in a moment of weakness,
wearing pince-nez, —
and they found me fashionable —

But what I wanted was for only a moment
to see things the way *they* do, to view matter
as perfection, without
any holes in it

            — and of course I donned pince-nez
not for stylish reasons, but for the simple fact
that I don't have any ears —

I abhor fashion. It's even worse
than having a personality.

Oh, I have many personae, they might say, —
but none of them are really *mine*, an immaculate order being
            for those who wish to exist
in the wrong kind of oblivion

my voices speaking through myriad voices, —
like when Emily Dickinson says
*I'm Nobody! Who are you?*

      it is not *her* speaking, but me,
through the vehicle of her voices.

I'm not stupid like they are.
And I'm not as cruel, either —

I possess enough integrity to survive, — and I don't
impose it upon others.

But from the beginning I've had many admirers, —
like the angels, after creation,
                              when they asked for their wings
to be studded with eyes — saying
they could bear witness more effectively
to all events of the world . . .

but really, they wanted to see things
the way *I* do. And they were suspicious
of their father.

If you examine their wings, like the wings
of bees, they shouldn't
be capable of flight

but they are.
They fly anyway.

IN PRAISE OF METAL
*(for Burke)*

I love the mood in a tin cup,
        because it's like the mood
in an abandoned building

the trussed latticework of bridges, —
on haunches perpetually,
                         feline
and on the verge of motion

At night when I go outside
                I bow to the stars
for being factories of metal

      I have a fantasy
      of being born
the way metal is born

to crawl saintly out of a fire, —
almost indestructible, with immense power

and yet without volition

      Metal in human hands has been used
for all imaginable deeds,
has expressed
every abstraction

whether shaped into electrum helmets
                worn by princes,
or Carolingian books of hours
of beaten gold
        inlaid with lapis lazuli

metal of weaponry, — of swords
and in the cogs of Roman chariots

                        metal
of hatred, in a terrible rain
into the Oto and Kyo rivers —

yet through it all, metal remains innocent —
it is our witness, — a catalog
of longing —


When I look at the most noble
and beautiful objects
wrought from metal
                  I sense they are fashioned
with a desire to capture essence, and for what is immortal
and unchanging

          Yet I say to be essential
is to rest in oblivion —
to be the form itself, —
and while the form of a magnificent object
is immortal, and unchanging,
                            we ourselves only forge them
through the most painful acts
of transformation

The metal we are most akin to then,
and what we must learn to love most of all
is the metal
which is falling away

     gold and silver dust
blown from the smithy's windows, —

    pewter worn away
from chess pieces —

   I would gather the metal lost
from old coins and keys,
      spiral bannisters

and from bands
around the ankles of women

and swans

Allow Charon if he should desire
to ferry my soul away,
   on that river running
into the amnesia of paradise

but I ask for my body to somehow be preserved, —
   I want if it is possible
     to be immersed in a molten lake
of all the lost metals of the world

And then place me at the gates of the city, —
     like the statues
mentioned in that poem by Lucretius

And I shall greet every traveller on their journey,
gazing out at them
with coldest eyes

witnessing all their deeds without judgement,
                    all the love and hatred
happening along the edge
of the highway

my one hand held out
        and grasped so often

        the metal will wear away
until the bones of my fingers show through

        my other hand
held up eternally
in that gesture of hello

and goodbye

goodbye and goodbye

AN OMNIGRAVIS

OMNIGRAVIS
(for Lewis and Maryla)

> And whence they came and whither they shall go
> The dew upon their feet shall manifest.
> — Wallace Stevens

I.

The submerged heart,
                        the spider drinking blood
in her underwater bell

each drop possessed of many motions,
                                her sad heart
            spins an omnigravis, — each silky thread
a memory of having fallen,
                      pulled tight and finely twisted


                O thin-veined sorrow, straining
from the centre of the earth

in her denuded, frozen mouth
                      that stillness

a stillness lying heavily on the pond.


II.

Know her mouth and sadness as your own, —
a sadness of the body,
                      beneath the violent
and secondary waters of the mind

remember a life sitting quietly,
     a medieval cloister
where you wove the finest lacework
in the world: — each turn of bobbin
an orison to a bridegroom

    a god you thought only lived
in the emptiness between threads

    Remember how the pope
adored you for your lace,
  but how you never left your room

married to half of something

    and how your hands could be seen
stretching out your window at night,
your pale, widow-thin hands

  hands that once longed to touch
a bare-faced moon —
its infinite mantilla of stars.


III.

Fall into a mood along her brow, a passion
shifting endlessly in her mouth

    fall along ropes of flesh,
flesh which is the primary
substance of your world

Let this soothe her heavy heart,
which is also your heart

                              and know your loneliness
as you walk through cities

their burnished tectonics of iron and glass

            unmoving cities, fashioned with wild hands
                        which sought a stillness
on the edge of every spire

while the mind raged, a mechanical bird
against the body's heavy bars


Remember walking through the broken cities
a question and answer,
                        their tireless embrace
among many large notions and abstractions

remember the charred bodies of Rome


Urge her to sound in the dark with you falling, —
            carry her to the centre
of the burning city

cradle the body adorned with fire — its last memory
                        of being one of many forgotten saints,
            a saint who knows
every argument is a lie,
                        that the city was a lie


As her blood burns beyond movement
O passion,
            O honesty of motion

it is for blood itself we die

THE FULCRUM OF FLIGHT
(for Bernice Friesen)

The young Michaelangelo,
                      searching
for stone in the quarry,
the Italian birds at dusk

singing their plain arias

He is drawn to a piece of rough marble;
it thinks he has interesting hands.

He ponders it for a long time,
the birds high above him,
                      each push of blood
at the centre

the heart, the fulcrum of flight

O to know the stone's private architecture,
                      its shibboleth
of sweep and arch

the Madonna unfolding from the vein: —


    Because this kind of patience
is the beginning of integrity — you can live your life
for this kind of waiting

            the trees at dusk
holding ravelled tendrils of light,
the birds fluttering around them

with their beaks open,
>                    *Madonna*

the stone speaking
before you hew it

the breath

the idea clotting into sound

HALF UNFOLDED

March is a goblin market,
                a conspiracy
                between memory and desire —

the mind of the sun in early spring
the infant's mind,
rowing slowly through the birth canal

        Imagine the pain it feels
as it dismantles its utopias — and then
swan dives into ignorance, disbelief,
                        which it musn't fail to do
in order that it might endure.

      The river's ice breaks apart
          into floes so fragile
they would sink with the weight of a mouse, —
                  or a mouse's desire
to cross a moving body of water

Every other tree on the bank possesses a magpie —
they remain regardless of the season,
                    portraying themselves
as if perpetually on the brink
of emerging from the underworld

        each bird's wings
pages of empty sheet music,
              with hearts
which are plums
throbbing in glasses of absinthe

The sun shines and gutters
                and then thunder gathers
over the retreating snow

        You imagine magpies
resting easily on the floes

laughing themselves
into states of weightlessness

This is what you do to get through spring.
Throw an anchor out into some limbo, and then be
neither here nor there, —
                        half unfolded
                        into light.

RODIN'S *EVE*
(*the* AGO, *Toronto*)

     You wept for such immeasurable light
— chained to pale stone —
gracious

     and fluid like a soft, slow
sarabande of snow

        You could weep
for much less than this, never considering
                     how it would be

     to bite into the promise
of godhood, that small
red galaxy


To wake with the pangs of blood,
             your lover fallen beside you
his lips bright, the first accusation

Kneeling then, upon the threshold between
                     two kinds of paradise

To the right of you,
             the angels with their hair burning

— angels in rapid order around a god —

   and to the left the wide sky,
          the most tangible trees

the pomegranates that hang there like hearts,
    all of them waiting
to live inside your mouth

and how you kneel there forever,
in the light, —
   at once holding,
       and refusing the light.

THE NATIVITY
(Geertgen tot Sint Jans, circa 1490)

Darkness and para-darkness
in the newborn's eyes

Pangaea brewing in the fontanel

    Already her mouth locked with sorrow
the round-faced Virgin,
              leaning into the light of her child: —

Her shoulders gather the weight. Every pieta
is a foreshadow garnered on dark cloth,

                        in momentary rest
                        from tragedy —

But the presence is known,
    viewed by the angels here
who sometimes glance beyond her shoulders
and kneel
as in a house of mourning

Angels with the faces of young girls,
                      who bear witness
to the dark flood at the beginning

They also lean, into this first light, —
the child who is a beacon,
                  whose eyes
are the dim heart of every star

They hold her sorrow
and the sorrow that will come —

Breathlessly they kneel in the barn —
to watch time being reborn —

They want to catch hold of him
as he is broken into every world.

THE HERMIT

I. *What He Would Want*

To be silent,
>without weight

like the grouse in her snowshoes
or a systolic moon

empty of blood at last

>and then to wait for his own light

to fill the darkness.


II. *Where He Lives*

Hermitage in the hills,
a place even the ice overlooked
>as it crawled down the face

of the continent

>his blood shackled always

in horsetail and long grasses

a desire to be invisible

apprentice to ghost, — salamander's acolyte, —
seeking anything that might dwell
in hidden alcoves of stone

he walks the dinosaur ossuary
humming its three-chambered song

>He follows the veins of a green river

wondering where it unfurled —
its private source,
>its mesozoic tributary

lying somewhere beneath the unbroken hills

III. *What She Loves About the Hermit*

Because he understands his soul
is half angel's,
           that almost nothing
like moonlight
refracted through a ghost, yet carrying
the world

half *afarensis*,
           its mantle of wills —
           that this is what the runners in Laetoli
were running to — the light in this lantern

the argument in every one of us —
           that dialectic
never exhausted through the millenia.

Because his heart is the den of an albino fox
in constant fear of summer

its diaphanous eyes,
           the unbridled
word between its teeth

the infrared flowers
it pulls from the blood

    She loves the cranial bowers
with their nacreous-fleshed angels,
           their mouths
always half-opened with a question

the winding corridors, the locked doorways, —
the high transoms she might fly through.

Every unfinished room in his mind.

ROSA ANIMAE

The rose of the soul is grey, —
                              its petals
fumulus gathered to a shape.  Unfolding
from a calyx ashen and still
                        holding silence
the way a bowl holds silence — buried
in a woman's arms at Pompeii —

    But it has never know the burden
of the particular —
                        though birds fly aloft
in its pigeon-grey sky, below them
it stands like a naked body

in a semblance of being veiled: —

And the birds fly to and fro,
each and each the same.
                        They are merely the form
a bird embraces
when it doesn't have a name.


The rose is never vertical, within
                        the moment

Its stem bears two thorns, —
one of memory,
one of presentiment, —

The rose of the soul witnesses judgement in a blur.
        Almost conceiving it
from pure understanding — it watches
from its tower the passing world.

Draped in grey wind, the last exhalations
of the living

        it is thrown back and forth
from the beginning until the end
and back to the beginning again, —

        and like a mirror
        wherever
        the rose of the soul is carried

whatever it inhabits, — it is always
entirely itself.

NOTES AND ACKNOWLEDGEMENTS

Quotations dispersed throughout the book are taken from the following poems:

Zbigniew Herbert, from "Five Men"; W.B. Yeats, from "The Phases of the Moon"; Rumi, from "Moses and the Shepherd"; Emily Dickinson, from "I'm Nobody! Who are you?", poem 288 (*The Complete Poems of Emily Dickinson*, edited by Thomas H. Johnson) and "I had been hungry, all the Years — ", poem 579; Wallace Stevens, from "Sunday Morning".

In section II of *Lessons for the Body*, the italicized lines are from T.S. Eliot's poem *Ash Wednesday*.

---

The *fovea centralis* is a depression at the back of the eye where light converges.

*Fabula Cygnorum* means, "A Story of Swans" or fable or tale. *Luna saltatoris* means "dancer's moon".

In the poem "I Shall Never Describe", "metamorphoses" is pronounced with a hard "p" and the "es" as "ayz" as in classical Latin.

The word "intraphysicum" in the poem "In the Rind" I would define as the thinnest shoal on the surface of *things*, which nonetheless possesses so many arabesques that it inhabits more space than the actual *body* of an object.

In "Through Light" the Latin translated into English means, "I have been singing to you across time. Through light. I want to put your name in my mouth. But it is everywhere. O radiance of absence! I have entered your light."

In the poem "A Short Gothic Tale", *matreshka* are Russian stacking dolls painted to resemble peasant women.

Mr. Cogito is a character created by Zbigniew Herbert

*Liber Ecstatis* — "Book of Ecstasy".

In the poem "Outdoor Chess", the image of the refugee with the silver cup (but not the lace) was stolen accidentally from a poem by Adam Zagajewski.

An *omnigravis* is the sorrow that comes after the fall.

*Rosa Animae* — "Rose of the Soul".

In the poem "The Hermit", *afarensis* is *Australopithecus afarensis*, a hominid first unearthed in Ethiopia's Afar Triangle in 1974 by Donald Johanson. Although there is still much debate, it is thought by many that *afarensis* walked in an upright posture, between 3 and 4 million years ago. Laetoli is the site in Tanzania where in 1978 Mary Leakey found hominid footprints which are dated at 3.5 million years old, attributed to belonging to *afarensis*. The footprints were made possible by the eruption of Sadiman, a nearby volcano. Its ash was rained on and then eventually hardened, leaving tracks of animals and hominids. It is thought that the hominids stopped briefly and looked west, perhaps to admire a sunset. The footprints are now covered and have been permanently damaged by weather and the roots of plants growing into them.

---

I'd like to thank the Saskatchewan Arts Board and The Canada Council for generous grants which gave me time to write these poems.

My gratitude as well to the editors of the following journals in which some of these poems appeared: *Arc, The Canadian Forum, Canadian Literature, The Fiddlehead, Grain*, and the anthology *Vintage '97/'98* (Quarry Press).

Thank you to Thistledown Press, Don Domanski for editing and his enthusiasm, and also Seán Virgo for ongoing support.